ADMIRATION FOR CHOO 3T FISH

"You cannot understand the arc of the arts in the last-half of the 20th Century without a thorough grounding in the poetry of Choo 3T Fish."
— RICHARD BLEDSOE, NATIONAL POET LAUREATE

"[Choo 3T Fish is] one of the most determined and inventive decomposers of contemporary American verse."
— JACK AMBER, POETRY NOW!

"The master of the short-form is most certainly Choo 3T Fish, the avant-gardist from Rhode Island. His flash-poems are blunt, and they strike quickly. Unlike those of the anti-artists or Dadaists at the turn of the last century, with whom he is often compared, his poems have a concussive quality, daring you to climb back to your feet, re-focus your eyes, and read another."
— JACQUE JAUNE, FROM THE NORTON ANTHOLOGY OF MODERN POETICS

"*Roe Roe Roe Your Boat* is as fresh as it is salty. It is blue seas under blue skies."
— D. J. LOUP, THE OREGON TIMES

"There is a surrealist flavor to [Choo 3T Fish's] poetry, of course, and an absurdist quality, too. But at heart these poems are deeply confessional, the poet's protestations notwithstanding. How can they not be, when every poem is filled with fish."
— THOMAS RUFF, PLOUGHSHARERS QUARTERLY

"I have taught the poetry of Choo 3T Fish to both adults and children. The adults struggle through each turn of phrase, and every fish must be carefully deboned, as if they're afraid *this* is the one they will finally choke on and die. The children? They just laugh and laugh. They get it."
— WALLY POLLOCK, POETRY JOURNAL NW

"*Swimming through the Darkness* was the first collection of poetry that made me want to tear out the pages and pin them to my wall. Nothing of his work doth fade, but doth suffer a sea-change into something rich and strange."
— DR. SUSAN HAUTALA, IRIDIUM

"He's like Honoré de Balzac, but shorter, sharper, Chinese, American, and with tremendous balls of fish."
— VAN JARAM, AUTHOR OF *GROWING UP BEATNIK*

"[Choo 3T Fish's] poetry is an acquired taste. Something between Brussels sprouts and toxic waste. His words are wet and lewd and chaste — there's nothing he won't lay to waste. Grab this book with utmost haste."
— IVOR SOSNOFF, *ARCHIVES OF INHUMAN POETRY*

"It is impossible to find a referent for the unremitting longing and lightness communicated in *Will You Hold My Breath*, an absolutely magnificent apotheosis of the salty verse of carnal desire."
— DASH HILARY, *THE NEW YORK TIMES*

"A maestro of the lyrically pickerel."
— JENDER WILMANN, *REVUE LITTERAIRE DE CANNES*

"To dip into [Choo 3T Fish's] poems is to dip into buoyancy and boisterousness, into a profound sense of spectacle and melancholy: *from the abyss i gently rise!*"
— RON QUIL, AUTHOR OF *NIT ONE PEARL TWO*

"America's most redoubtable poet."
— S C M HAMMER, FROM *ALTERNATING CURRENTS*

Also by Choo 3T Fish

A POCKETFUL OF FISH

Choo 3T Fish

Edited by

Mark Malamud and Tamara Croup

for Cary

A POCKETFUL OF FISH

Copyright © 2019 by Mark Malamud
Cover art © 2019 "Toronado" by Sudhir Bansal

Third Regulus Press printing June 2021
Wobble Library 00-1202-30-40

Regulus Press, Seattle WA
www.regulus.press

ISBN: 0999446215
ISBN-13: 978-0-9994462-1-8 (Regulus Press)

When the last fish is caught,
we will realize we can't eat money.

— Native American proverb

If you judge a fish by its ability to climb a tree,
it will live its whole life believing that it is stupid.

— Albert Einstein

All men are equal before fish.

— Herbert Hoover

Fish don't shoot back. Fish shoots back.

— Choo 3T Fish

Foreword

ALL TOO OFTEN I find myself in the company of someone who is unfamiliar with Choo 3T Fish — "Who?" I'm asked bluntly, usually before a swift change of subject.

I anticipate such ignorance from my American undergraduates for whom a primary education in Western poetry consists almost exclusively of William Shakespeare and e. e. cummings, as if from those points one might wholly reconstruct the span of English-language poets between them, as if this minimal geometry were sufficient for a student to cross the chasm of expressive illiteracy; — yet it is still unacceptable. Worse is when I encounter a young adult, putatively well-read, who despite being a man (or woman) of letters is woefully unprepared to discuss contemporary poetry; or, worse still, a contemporary who — despite having lived through the tumultuous Fifties and Sixties when the assault on tradition threw heavenward another generation of major poets: Ginsberg, Burroughs, Kerouac, Bukowski, even Dylan and the Beatles — is wholly ignorant of one of the brightest stars in that firmament of our generation of "great and modern" North American poets: Choo 3T Fish.

Why *he* has been relegated to the heap of nearly forgotten poets is impossible to say. Like Bukowski, his work can be direct and grotesque. Like Baldwin, it is laser-focused on a personal experience of racism. Like Kerouac, it is an energetic palliative against yearning and loss. Like Ginsberg, it is infused with an alienated sexuality. His poetry is, among other things, lyrical, vigorous, challenging, erudite, confessional, erotic, illuminating ... *sui generis*.

So perhaps, in the end, it *is* all about the fish.

Zhu Fish (奇怪的鱼) was born in the Feng Tien Province of China, ca. 1928. His parents, both academicians, fled the country shortly before the nationalist government set up in Nanjing. His father, Zheng Heyu Fish (鄭和魚), moved the family first to Singapore, then Tonkin in North Vietnam, and in 1936 to the Lower East Side of Manhattan where the young Zhu was enrolled in a small "mixed-race" grammar school just off Houston Street to learn English. The following year he was accepted into the Horace Mann School (formerly of Columbia University) on a "war-provisions" scholarship, where, despite his having published in its literary magazine seventeen poems over six years, few remember him from the Class of '46.

Reading one of those early poems, "Feeling Vague" [*Horace Mann Manuscript*, Spring, 1941], it's not particularly hard to understand why:

> *I am a carrier of plague,*
> *They say; a yellow fellow,*
> *Just look at my skin. Cette nouvelle vague*
> *Is original sin. My eyes are like gill slits;*
> *I could be drowning in the sea;*
> *Wave, and no one would rescue me.*
> *Wave, and no one would even see.*

On 19 February 1942, President Roosevelt signed Executive Order 9066, and shortly thereafter young Zhu Fish learned that his parents, travelling in Colorado, were to be "temporarily detained" in a Wartime Civil Control Administration Assembly Center, a euphemism for *internment camp* — itself a euphemism for *concentration camp*. It's not known why as Chinese Americans they were imprisoned along with the Japanese (although given the despicable history it is sadly unsurprising), and for nearly ten months. Meanwhile, at home, the covert racism of his first years of high school turned overt, with disruptions and fist-fights documented in his school transcript. Although his parents returned early in 1943, the damage was significant: his mother succumbed to pulmonary tuberculosis later that year, and by the time "Zhu Choo Fish" was graduated from Horace Mann *magna cum laude* with honors, his father had died of a hemorrhagic stroke.

A scholarship from Princeton University took him to New Jersey, although an unremarkable transcript suggests disengagement, if not neglect, during this period. Indeed, he remained unpublished throughout his college years: later poems refer obliquely to an academic journey filled with "southern depressions" and "uncivil rites." In 1955, he returned to New York as a part-time Professor at Fordham University in the Bronx, where he published his only collection of academic essays, *A Grotesque Aberration: Transitions and Change from the People's Volunteer Army to the Standoff at Shantou* [Department of Asian Studies, Fordham Press, 1955], six rather dry and dreary critiques of China at the beginning of the Mao Era. More interesting is the epigrammatic poetry he placed throughout the mid-to-late Fifties in small newspapers throughout the metropolitan area, including *The Brooklyn Eagle, Robotnik*

Polski, and the nascent *Village Voice*.

In "Keep Calm and Carrion" [*New York Herald Tribune*, 1957], a free-verse confection built from alternating trochaic and iambic rhythms, he writes:

> *Until I can teach you*
> *I know nothing*
> *You will learn nothing.*
>
> *Forget wisdom and learning;*
> *Try ambiguity and yearning.*

In 1962, modifying his name for the last time, "Choo 3T Fish" joined the Harvard Graduate School of Arts and Sciences with a special interest in the avant-garde. His first collection of poetry, *I Am Not Fish*, was published by Harvard Press in 1964. Although the primary subject was the racism Fish experienced throughout his childhood and adolescence, the predictable severity of the topic was offset by a style suggestive of a parody of formal poetry, with allegories and near-rhymes used to subvert both the seriousness of theme as well as the expectations of line-breaks and meter.

For example, in "my skin is dry" [*I Am Not Fish*, Harvard Press, 1964], he writes:

> *This name, bar sinister, this Tat*
> *too Is no more me*
> *than i am you, Than*
> *i am in the water. blue, Swimming*
> *through*
> *beat me And i will not cry*
> *beat me Now my skin is dry*

In 1984, Choo 3T Fish wrote of this first collection: "I was struggling at the time with the affectations of what I called 'meaningless meaninglessness' explicit in so many of the poets, specifically the Beat [Generation] poets, whom I admired, nonetheless. What I wanted to find was a way to embrace a similar aesthetic yet without the implications of that same weaselly & measly playfulness, so when I understood I might exploit the tension between expectation and manifestation to mirror the reality dysfunction I experience as the target of visible racism, of the conflict between who I am and who I am perceived to be, I knew I had stumbled onto a burlesque form I could bend to my will" [*Periodicity*, Winter, 1985]. And indeed this was a formula he would continue to work throughout his career, even if this initial collection — as Choo 3T Fish liked to joke — "didn't make much of a splash" [*ArtVOID*, Spring, 2000], possibly due to its being released the same week as Allen Ginsburg's *Reality Sandwiches.*

Choo 3T Fish continued to compose, of course, and with his second collection, *Incidentally Underwater* [Harvard Press, 1965], it was clear his purpose was not to express a point of view but also to deconstruct it. "I want to understand why we write, perhaps more than what we write," he said in 1966, shortly after assuming the title of assistant professor in Harvard's College of the Littoral Arts. "I want the reader to ask why, always why." [*Collected Letters*, John Hay Library, Brown University, 1970].

Although his work would return on occasion to issues of race and racism, it was clear upon the publication of his second collection that he was ready to push the boundaries of acceptable poesy beyond figurative confession. Most of the poems in *Incidentally Underwater* are inverted narratives, reconstructions of an imperfect ballad stanza with the first and third lines in each stanza being an iambic trimester, and the second and fourth lines being iambic tetrameter, a simple reversal of the traditional Romantic form used by William Wordsworth. The poet is hidden, submerged, and yet the poetry is alive with personality and concern. "Tell all the truth but tell it slant." The lines are elliptical, but severe, emphatic. Shadows jingle and clatter, colors sing, in an psychedelic explosion of synesthesia. The mistakes in meter are unconcealed and purposeful, but it's the last six lines of the collection, in "aweigh anchor," that make it clear he'd set a fresh direction for himself, that *Incidentally Underwater* was no less than a port of departure, and he was prepared to embark:

> *because everything is why [therefore] everything is why not*
> *i won't take [you] anywhere you want*
> *to go i'll take [you] everywhere*
> *the ocean's high, and [the time of fish] is nigh*
>
> *this anger, this anchor, aweigh—*
> *away! away! away! away! away! away!*

Despite this manifesto of urgency, this buoyant and desperate *bon voyage*, it would take Choo 3T Fish a decade to publish his third volume of poetry. Not because he wasn't writing — the Fish Archives at Brown University contain *sixteen thousand* pages of his work from that decade. No, it was because he'd set off to an unknown destination, and it took him that long to recognize when he'd arrived. And arrive he did: *Swimming through the Darkness* [Harvard Press, 1974] was not only a masterpiece of American verse, but it also marked the beginning of a remarkable thirty-year run of piscatorial poetry that was both form-defining and genre-defying.

The three books in this omnibus collection were published within those astonishing thirty years of the poet's life. These are the trusted sources, drafted in consultation with the poet's agent, C. M. Barnett, as well as with Fish expert Mark Malamud with whom the present volume is co-edited.

Selecting which books would best represent the poet wasn't easy. *Swimming through the Darkness*, recipient of numerous accolades including the National Poetry Award in 1974, would have to be included, of course, as well as its follow-up collection, *Roe Roe Roe Your Boat*, containing "born on a ripple" and "call me fish meal." But selecting the third book posed a significant challenge. Should it provide an amplification to the other selections, or a counter-point? We considered *Fish Fish Fish Fish Fish,* with its fourteen elegiac poems cataloging over four-thousand varieties of fish; as well as *Dioscuri Towers*, in which the poet abandons the life aquatic for only the second time (instead focusing on the September 11th terrorist attack: "sophoclean particulates punctuate each breath / you'll believe a muslim can fly").

In the end, we determined neither extremity offered what we hoped to accomplish with this new publication: a representative yet accessible introduction to the work of "America's most redoubtable poet" [*Alternating Currents: The Contradictions of Choo 3T Fish*, S C M Hammer, 1984]. Thus we narrowed our final selection to four candidates, all published between 1980 and 2000 during which the poet was an active professor at Brown University and a notable personality throughout Providence, Rhode Island. This period is distinguished by a profligate burst of creativity, much of which was eclipsed at the time by the turbulent personal life of the poet that included an affair with the wife of a mobster mayor, an arrest on drug charges, heart surgery, and an extended stay at "that *petit mouchoir*" in the south of France where he was held prisoner for nearly eight months in the castle of the Teutonic "mad Alsatian" publisher Deckard Gerhardt. (Although a distressing period of his life, the incarceration raised his profile in France where he is considered, even today, an adoptive national treasure, one of several distinctly American imports, including Jerry Lewis, Philip K. Dick, and Disco Rigido.) *King Me* is a dark and challenging collection that focuses on that time of incarceration — atmospheric, but wholly without a single signature fish; *Upstream Fornication* and *$ushi* followed, describing his liberation from France and his subsequent return to America; and finally, *Will You Hold My Breath*, a tender collection of epithalamic poetry. After considerable debate, we agreed that

Breath was the most uplifting of these lesser-known volumes, and a powerful — and romantic — return to form. Many of the poems were a revelation to readers whose familiarity had never strayed beyond the poet's most popular canon; and they include the intertwining of Sappho, Shakespeare, and Jesus in equal measure. Oh, and fish, of course.

This omnibus collection is long overdue. If you're one of those for whom the name Choo 3T Fish has been a cipher or a void — you're in for a treat. If you're already familiar with his work, we hope you find this omnibus an opportunity to expand the horizons of your appreciation. In 2005, the Poet Laureate Authority to the Library of Congress, Richard Bledsoe, wrote, "You cannot understand the arc of the arts in the last-half of the 20th Century without a thorough grounding in the poetry of Choo 3T Fish." Perhaps, at last, the "time of fish" has arrived.

Tamara Croup

Saint John University, Lebanon
5 September 2018

Fish Is Fowl and Fowl Is Fish

A New Introduction by the Poet

I WON'T TELL YOU what happened.

I won't tell you what happened when I became an orphaned adult or when my brother by another mother and father reclined into a limbless deathless slumber; or when I awoke to my own screams in the center of the night, to my bed sheets soaked in sweat, to the chest pain and scarcity of breath, to the deep vein thrombosis and the subsequent pulmonary embolism. I won't tell you about the numerable losses — of lovers and love, hairs on my head, heart, hope, antipathy; or the words that were forgotten or recalled, or mislaid, or misunderstood, poems forsaken, books unpublished; or that time during the late afternoon when agèd and hoary I'd learned I'd become "overnight" a "grand-master" poet, recognized and acknowledged, and I ran over dune and down to shore, dipping my tiny twisted toes into trembling riptides, limp, drizzly, out of oxygen, hopeless — or hopeful, it doesn't matter which. I won't tell you about Katerina or Pam or Milosevic or Josh. I won't tell you about the flatcar, or my return to the castle, or the break-in. I won't tell you how I felt, or feel, or will feel. I won't illuminate my interior, just as I would never darken your doorstep. I won't exhibit my exterior, or show my posterior, or share my familiar. I won't tell you any of this because it is middle-of-the-majority life, grubby life, quotidian life, unplanned indiscriminate unsystematic life, my life, of no inherent interest to you, whether petty triumphs or elemental peccadillos that I might otherwise pen in letters melodramatic, paint in colors vivid, or sing in voice operatic, in timbres symphonic, or melodies pop, faking beauty and novelty, feigning import and interest, thrilling you; and no doubt you'd swoon and I'd catch you in my arms, kisses hither and yon, but it is all faux, fast food to go, to go go go go go go go, to be gone. I won't tell you any of it, and I hope I never have and I never will.

Instead, I won't tell you what happened. Inside each book — *Swimming through the Darkness, Roe Roe Roe Your Boat, Will You Hold My Breath* — on every page, in every poem, in line after line or word after word, in the presence or absence of capitals and marks of punctuation, goddammit praise the lord hail satan I'll resist the urgency of explanation, of explication, of trust; I'll resist the urge to pull the wool over your eyes, to pull the wool over your head, to unbutton your blouse, unzip your pants, root around, poke and prod, kiss, lick, and suckle until you scream; I won't let you go and I won't let you come; and instead, in recompense, I won't tell you what happened and I never will.

Instead, I'll share the abyss from which there is no escape. This abyss, right here, in my hospital bed. This involution ocean, all around us. The blood of the covenant is thicker than the water of the womb, sicker than the water of the sea. We are born in water, borne and carried by water, die in water. Seriously, why did you think there were so many fish?

This book, this omnibus, this collection of "ichthyopathic poetry" is in your hands now. Appeal to Heaven — or Hell — it won't do any good, and might do harm. So why not just enjoy yourself. The water is cold. Fish is hot. Come on in.

Choo 3T Fish

Miriam Hospital, RI
30 October 2018

A POCKETFUL OF FISH

SWIMMING
THROUGH THE DARKNESS

CHOO 3T FISH

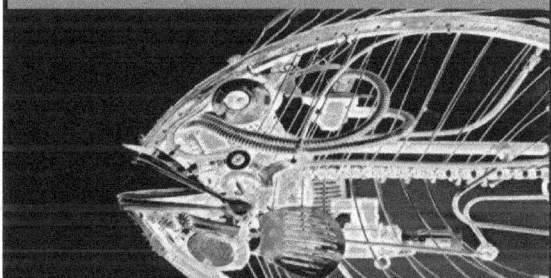

Overleaf

Reproduction of the cover from the second edition, published by Harvard Press, Boston, 1974.
Artwork by Gimo Carolle. Commissioned by Alexina Trekbecl.

CONTENTS

her movements gentle as the day

her movements gentle as the day
her teeth as white
she keeps her thoughts
she laughs at haddock

invisible pain

we did it when we were kids
and we never found out why

the invisible pain

now the bread in my hand is blurry
this new pair of glasses

this new prescription
sucks

you gave me these
when i didn't say goodbye

and now i can't see for shit
faces, commas, the sky

indistinct, hazy, obscure
why is it that the only things

in focus now are
six feet away

sometimes with a rite of passage you have a drink
a martini, a glass of wine, even a beer

now maybe just a bowl of soup, or fish stew
six feet under

i meant six feet under

invisible pain (au chocolat)

there is a game i'd like to play with you
in that dour patisserie in gay paris

with boys with boys and girls with girls
god bless you — *geworfenheit*

when you're dead and you can't talk back
when you're ghostly and wraithlike and vague

it goes like this: you sit there and watch me
and i open my mouth wide

and i pretend to raise a chocolate croissant to my lips
and i stuff it into my mouth and make fake chewing sounds

then i suck on my finger mmmm
like i'm sucking on you

"you know what you just ate?"
in that dour patisserie in gay paris

when somehow you still just won't shut up
a raw slab of frozen tusk fish

petting, posting the bands

petting, posting the bands
nuptial bond, matrimony
the married knot, spooning and cooing
groom and bride, not until death
holy wedlock, wedded bliss

man sleeps in pairs
but all fish sleep together

my love is like a dying rose

my love is like a dying rose
and
my love is like betraying me
and
the window opens up her beauty
and
the window opens down her red grace
and
i try to escape her thighs
but
i go to the kitchen and eat raw flounder instead

i was fashionably late for bed

i was fashionably late for bed
and
i waited, breathing your air
and
father
i waited, hoping you'd tell me
to fuck a wet salmon

love tuna wobble-wobble

you dance to me
you dance to pleasure
as
i see your face
i rush to the bakery
and
if
we do
love tuna wobble-wobble

sea thoughts, or sea mail

sea thoughts, or sea mail terrifies

each twist and turn
in blue-green skies her waves as
smooth as mermaids' thighs

paddle-backward
through tempests wise to hide our
salty tears, good-byes

my hand is open, seaweed
cries, "from the abyss
i gently rise!"

between my toes a star fish sighs

they buried me uncooked

they buried me uncooked
without an erection
in a coffin filled with fish
on the wrong side of town
a raw deal
but still
a good buy
fish

and indeed there will be time
to wonder, "do i dare?" and, "do i dare?"

and the air
fills the vacuum
left by my departure
with only a whisper
shhh

Internal epigraph from
"The Love Song of J. Alfred Prufrock" by T. S. Eliot

sea grass continues to grow

freedom and liberty the pavane dance
and
war and peace on settee recline
and
time and tide bathe in shoals of chance
while past and future buck the divine
but
sea grass continues to grow
and
power tools fool the mightiest squid

nine i am not a flying fish

nine minutes to monday
eight hours to dawn
seven sorrows to capture
six passes to pawn
five minutes to kiss
four hours to pray
three flimsy raptures
two unholy, delay
one fish, flying
sailing, away

A Soviet first strike launched from submarines off the East Coast
will take less than nine minutes to reach their
targets in the continental U.S.

take birth and death

take birth and death
and love and locks
and doors and shysters
and pills and rocks

nothing makes sense
until
you dream

of a frosty magnum
of tippled trout

poison fish

i asked myself to work
i asked myself to play
and slowly, slowly

i asked myself to meter out a mild invective
i asked myself to pretense
i asked myself to grovel

really, another lap around the deck?
like a wave at the shore
like a dog at his mistress
like a poison fish

— strike that! the sailor cried
(he who walks, also rans)

pterois volitans

the size of things to come is small

the size of things to come is small
and the size of things to come is quiet
and i hold you in my hand
and the sound of your breath
the thought of your hunger
a tentative turn
keeps my world dancing jetés
in quanta quiet and small

got any sues? (i won't tell)

— go fish

for SLH

inverted sock

inverted sock
triumphal march
first baptist meeting house
van wickle gates
baccalaureate
commencement
honorary degree
rain plan
graduates
bears
procession
cap and gown

a raw fillet of mackerel
tucked under your arm

For the Graduation Commencement Address,
Brown University, 1972.

shoaling and schooling

the vast and the furious
stay together for social reasons
majestic, everlasting
swimming in the same direction

one quarter of fish species
shoal all their lives
and about one half
shoal for part of their lives

and the rest?
they're schooled and they sink
to the sandy bottom of the sea
between the valley of shadows

they're schooled and they sink
to the sandy bottom of the sea
between the mountains of madness
dormant, uncharted

to the sandy bottom of the sea
between the whispers of shell fish
great and unexplored
sullen and blue-black

in a coordinated manner for five hundred years
your god-damn husband is away, and then he reappears

a fish is a bird of the sea

a fish is a bird of the sea
like a bird is a fish of debris
rising from the abyss

come now, sailor, come with me
open your eyes, dive deep, and see
my topography

a shadow mountain
a patch of red in void
a fiery funnel of light

spewing mud into the night
sky salty ocean deep
and from those ashes

a fledgling phoenix rises
sopping wet

swimming through the darkness

swimming through the darkness
longing for a light
a cigarette hangs
from your lips
like the useless tongue of an untrustworthy grouper

a watery grave

the sea is a cemetery of fish
for fish; a womb
to fish; a watery grave
in a salty boudoir
where salmon fornicate upstream
before dying, flapping in the arms of a fat woman
with a gun in a holster and a bottle of beer
whose pee turns the open ocean yellow
tang longhorn
cowfish moo

ROE
ROE
ROE
YOUR
BOAT

CHOO 3T FISH

Overleaf

Reproduction of the cover from the first edition, published by Harvard Press, Boston, 1978. Artwork by Daniel Isodore. Commissioned by Annie May Dawn.

CONTENTS

s/alt 1-6

s/alt 1: more salt

more salt
more sea
and
more cake
morey

amsterdam
new york
a comedian is neither
a moray eel on a hook nor

an afternoon sport
aqueous humor is salty
humor is

off-color, ribald,
vulgar, boorish, lewd,

wet

s/alt 2: more salt than thyme

more salt than thyme
more hope than rhyme
more salt more sea
more sleep than thee
more curds than whey

the hour points the tiny hand
towards fish that walk upon the sand

s/alt 3: salt rises in sunlight

salt rises in sunlight
then night falls, undulates
as
the ground beneath
the drowned mountains
rages, storms, and swallows
a tidal wave of carp

s/alt 4: there's nothing wrong with salt

there's nothing wrong with salt
more salt more sea
a herring smelt, nor
a season of brine
a drop of golden sun

from hope hidden in
opera — find me
that silent h, a
high c ladyfish,
and sing!

s/alt 5: roe roe roe

roe roe roe
your boat
your bloated boat
your stubby tube of joy
into this brackish pool of sand stake sex
my desires await
your attentions
my caviar
your milt
in my room
where every night is the same
my barrels are empty
but
my pistol is loaded

s/alt 6: count the clock

count the clock the son that set
the boy untimely ripped you let
him dip and sip and lick you wet
a taste of salt he won't forget
a wagered hungry birthing net
laid end to end a lover's debt

my pet, i'll fill your oceans deep
with seamen who will never sleep
with passions you will never keep
and children who forever weep

will creep upon the sandy shore
like crabs forlorn forever more

vigorous salty intercourse

call me fish meal

take a turn little doggie

take a turn little doggie
take a turn lest you grow
sadder than a cocker spaniel
wiser than the wisest know
take a turn little doggie
and let the seamen blow
your dinner starboard off the
listing mackerel bateau

the ocean is a babel of waves

the ocean is a babel of waves
the ocean is a story of shame
and expulsion
by day and night overlooking
the sea and the sand is
a tower of boozy monkfish

a chapel of waves
a history of shame
and expulsion
of day and night over
the sea and the sand is
a tower of bucket monks

the ocean is a chapel of gestures
the ocean is a history of disgrace
and expulsion
from day and night over
the sea and the sand
a tower of bucket monks

there is a chapel of sea gestures
there is a humiliation of history
and extraction
from day and night
sea and sand
a tower of dammar rabbit chum

such movements he prays
hide a shameful history
of amputation
day and night
sea and sand
a tower of dumbling urchin

the ocean is a babel of waves
tall-tale cacophony
horn bats and devil dogs
you won't forget me, will you?
in the churn of many waters
below a tower of boozy monkfish

the road is a four letter word

the road is a four letter word
too long without a brake
and
time exhausts you
a checkered flag
hot leather and high hopes
on the back of a stingray

For the Chevrolet Memorial Benefit Series,
Daytona Beach, 1976.

this is no time

this is no time for womb service, baby
this is a time to take the stairs

the elevator's not coming up
when the building's burning down

when everyone is racing to escape
when your body is a hotel

full of salt and water and fish
this is a time to check out, not in

this is a time for angst, not thanks
maybe we should just sit this one out

hell, no.
let's kick us some honky white ass

down the elevator shaft
and cod

In collaboration with N. D. King.

as a young child i saw you, as you hid

as a young child i saw you, as you hid
and
as a young child i slept in a bed
where i watched you, as you hid
and i slept
watching
waiting for you to mention fish

white waters

white
waters
red seas
hooks, lines,

and lures
and
never a wave

only a heavenly ripple
tightens a noose around the head of

an angelfish

blood is blue

i know your sleep is precious
i know your dreams are pure
and i know your blood is blue

i know your bells are silent
beneath your cotton sea
and i know your purpose even when
your porpoise keeps an eye on me

but
when
you awake
you will find
the romantic reconnoiter of
a warty angler in your pants

the fishermen, that walk upon the beach

VOLTIMAND

    The fishermen, that walk upon the beach,
    they're half fish, half flesh: a plague on them.
    These fishers tell the infirmities of men
    no more than a fish loves water. Is not this a
    being but half a fish and half a monster?

CORNELIUS

    No, they are both as whole as a fish.

VOLTIMAND

    But fish not, with this melancholy bait?
    Bait the hook well; this fish will bite.
    We'll have flesh for holidays, fish for
    ten thousand men that fishes gnaw'd upon;
    as ravenous fishes, do a vessel follow —

CORNELIUS

    I'll fish for thee and get thee wood enough.

VOLTIMAND

    Because I am so dwarfish and so low?
    "Help, master, help!" Here's a fish hangs in the net,
    is a plain fish, and, no doubt, marketable.
    Marvel how the fishes live in the sea —
    and make a stock-fish of thee.

CORNELIUS

    Excellent well; you are a fishmonger.

    CORNELIUS moves him to put on his hat.

VOLTIMAND

My opinion; hold it no longer: this is no fish,
was a fishmonger: he is far gone, far gone: and
to bait fish withal: if it will feed nothing else,
here's another ballad of a fish.

CORNELIUS

This is the news? He fishes, drinks, and wastes?

VOLTIMAND

A man may fish with the worm that hath eat of a
king, and cat of the fish that hath fed of that worm.
Whiles others fish with craft for great opinion,
of more preeminence than fish and fowls,
than baits to fish, or honey-stalks to sheep.

CORNELIUS

Henceforth eat no fish of fortune's buttering —

VOLTIMAND

Upon a dwarfish thief!
For a fish without a fin, there's a fowl without a feather,
as beasts and birds and fishes —

CORNELIUS

I —

VOLTIMAND

— And of a dragon and a finless fish,
drop and liquor fishermen's boots with me; I warrant
by fishermen of Corinth, as we thought,
tawny-finn'd fishes — my bended hook shall pierce!

CORNELIUS

That sort was well fished for.

VOLTIMAND

> As once I was, and had but this fish painted,
> as is the osprey to the fish, who takes it,
> as fish are in a pond. but now the bishop —
> why, she's neither fish nor flesh; a man knows not.

CORNELIUS

> The pleasant'st angling is to see the fish
> up fish street! Down saint magnus' corner! Kill
> the beasts, the fishes, and the winged fowls.

VOLTIMAND

> How art thou fishified! Now is he for the numbers
> grown a very land-fish, language-less, a monster!

CORNELIUS

> "Peace be at your labour, honest fishermen!"

> *CORNELIUS lifts scepter and kneels, then whispers aside.*

> He smells like a fish; a very ancient.

VOLTIMAND

> Did hang a salt-fish on his hook, which he
> cannot choose; and to eat no fish?
> Canst thou catch any fishes, then?

CORNELIUS

> Here? A man or a fish? Dead or alive? A fish.

> *Exeunt VOLTIMAND and CORNELIUS*

*For the RSC Recycling Festival,
Stratford-upon-Avon, 1972.*

the price of fish

the price of fish is high
the price of fish is lonely
and for thy sweet love
remembered such wealth brings
that i'd scorn to change my state
with the gill-bearing aquatic craniate animals
that lack limbs with digits

when you fish

life is simple
upside down

up through water
you see sky

and then
later that night
when you fish
upon a star

catch and ripples
away

blowfish

a guppy and gulper walk into a bar
a lamprey and loach take their feelings too far
a seal and a smelt dance a tango for two
a whitebait and whiff cry, "oh barb! what to do?"

the sea is a shore of long hidden delight
where fish fret and love in the daytime of night
and the ship that sails sleepy over their heads
leaves and returns from dry land to sea beds

for love in the sea is like life on dry land
neither flipper nor fin will tease hand from hand
for love in the sea is like love in our hearts
a salty red plasma that stops and restarts

you know that the blowfish blows kisses brand new
wherever he is he is still loving you
the blowfish that whispers he whispers your name
the blowfish the blowfish the blowfish — the same

for SLH

blue fish

one fish
two fish
red fish
blue fish

blue fish
red fish
big fish
dead fish

borne on a ripple

borne on a ripple
borne on a wave

yet content to dine
on food that is
always soggy

i am one hot piece of ass
i am the black sea bass

wanting (the anniversary of my death)

every year without knowing it I have passed the day
when the last fires will wave to me
and the silence will set out
tireless traveler
like the beam of a lightless star
across a resting sea
wanting what it cannot have —
fish

after W. S. Merwin

a deckhand who eats

there's a deckhand who eats
only fish skulls and ends
and he'll show you his teeth
that have suffered the bends
that can haul up the mains
that can rip them to rends
and he yells to the chef
with his arms at his side
"hey, bring me more trawl
to share with my bride"
and he wants so to die
but he's vain and he's high
so he stands up and sings
as he unzips up his fly
ing fish

after Jacques Brel

but a fisherman first

jesus walks along the edge of the sea
in shorts, bare-chested,
sandled feet, sandy hair,
serious

over his shoulder a long stick or pole
a bag of bait or lures on his hip
his eyes are not mediteranean blue
but his skin is the color of oil

extra virgin, a relative of lilac and jasmine,
brothers and sisters he has none,
a shepherd of the ocean, a poimen,
a puzzle, a masculine noun

power, action, bending curve
and tapering, he plants his feet
in the cold dark wet sand
and says

i shall rule them with a rod of iron,
but reel them with a rod of graphite,
carbon, fiberglass, and sometimes
bamboozle

a flat line cast out
to sea, a sign, a wave,
the kiss of death upon its lips
kiss me

by hook or by crook
i will put language
into your mouth and together
we will speak in barbed tongues

as i reel you in
as you gasp for breath
you may hope to be thrown
back into the abyss of tears

but you are deceived
for the sea is without air and
though you die on the shore
you will live forever

in me
remember

i am a fisher of men
but a fisherman first

bait and switch

unlike dice
fish have two sides
and one role

righteousness and whatever's left
they are dualists
not squares

mater and maw
take me in your hairy arms
take me on the shore

like a robe in the sea
you open for me
like a line in a wave

an only child
an oily fish
ground up and scattered

on the waters of the sea
a fin and claw
a bait and switch

i am enamored
with you, girl — littorally,
i am your chum

call me fish meal

i hunger for love
i hunger for time
yet over the hills

down to the shore
into the surf
the end of all songs

like a sea canary
in a cold mind
i cannot be re-imagined

look at me
dead in the water —
call me fish meal

WINNER OF THE NATIONAL POETRY AWARD

CHOO 3T FISH

will you
hold my
breath

COLLECTED POEMS

Overleaf

Reproduction of the cover from the first edition, published by Pembroke Press, Rhode Island, 1994. Artwork by Alison Lamb. Commissioned by the author.

CONTENTS

Author's Note

"Sea grass continues to grow" despite man's best efforts to arm against an imaginary sea of troubles. "Oh, very well, *set*," says the king to the sinking sun in one of Gahan Wilson's trenchant caricatures.

A writer is loath to speak in specifics about work that is by definition antagonistic to explanation. By definition each "brief narrative" is a battle between semantics and syntax, a kind of internecine warfare. But really its bigness is in its smallness, and I consider each poem a tiny living thing, a human thing, with a beating heart in conflict with itself, the only thing worth writing about. No one has a weak heart: each beat is an exercise of hope before loss. The heart in love is just the same. Muscle tension increases. Breathing accelerates. Hips rise. I have long refused to build on dry land. I live in the sea, by choice. Carl Jung suggests the sea is unconscious, abyssal, infinite, and empty; and we fill it with fish. *I* fill it with fish. We are the fish at least as much as we are the dead. George Orwell knew that. You can fuck in the ocean as you fuck on the earth. Sea grass continues to grow.

Art is never enough, though. I peddle fish I find in my net for a pittance. There are no other fish to fry. *These* are the fish I serve, for as long as I can. Unhappiness exposes happiness. It cannot be otherwise. Every happy fish is the same, but every unhappy fish is unhappy in its own way. And there are more fish, if only I have time to catch them. This is a collection, then, of love in the ruins, nakedness and fig leaves. *La langue* in French is both "language" and "tongue," and I wouldn't be much of a lover, or poet, without obeisance to each. Nam June Paik told me once, in a plosive of wonder: "Art is universal. It doesn't require explanation, good or bad. But Hollywood! It's the same thing, only with money!" I have medical bills, a mortgage, and a multiplicity of affluent addictions. Please, dear god, *help me*. Poetry, like love, is never enough. And, frankly, "loach goby hosts a vegetarian thanksgiving" would make a *terrific* blockbuster movie. Don't you think?

"…Oh, very well, *art*."

Choo 3T Fish

Providence, RI
31 August 1993

fin-

the seas weep constantly and grieve
heaving cold sorrows onto unforgiving shores
for the forlorn are forgotten

and the forgotten are no more
these tidal tears are given and gone,
misbegotten, melancholy, ill-conceived

ladyfinger, master plan,
a fine, a find, a finch
i am definitely

spoofing infinities
when i row out into the storm to find you
i glance over my shoulder

to see into the future
my end is in your love
while your picture is in davey jones' locker

every angel

every angel
an angle, a sing-song
every angel
agile, an anarchist

my breath grows short
my heart longs
and
your face flush
red snapper

to his coy dominatrix

had we but world enough and time
i might bother with internal rhyme
i might bother with syntax, too
and meaning, flowers, fingers new

if you were a rose in your prime
i might skip this crude pantomime
i might be tender, sweet, and true
and you might be less eager, too
had we but world enough and time

who would choose to grunt and sweat through
something so dreadful after death
as the undiscovered country
of your twisted toothless smile
the sagging lips and open mouth
from which no visitor returns

like a geriatric shark
we must keep moving, you say

several species, including humans

several species, including humans
are consumed as fish

throughout history
in fisheries and fisheries, fish

may contain magicks such as mollusks
crustaceans and echinoderms

english is no different for fish
no more than the animal and foods made therefrom

such as pork or beef
yet some other languages do so

such as spanish *pescado* or *pez*
a modern english word for fish

comes from an old english word *fisc*
covering the fish in the sea and the sea

in the air and the sea
you see from the shore, you know

there are several societies
whose men are eaten like a fish

throughout history
in fisheries and fisheries, english

is no different:
fork against fork, or reef against reef

food, fish and fish
like tentacles entwined, like lovers

of fish — and fishermen are just as nutritious
if they are prepared whole, and in many cases

they cannot be made in the form of
chokers and analgesic

lubricants and aphrodisiacs, hormones
and beta-carotene for dwindling the sex of fish

no, you must throw them down, peel
off their bright yellow rain gear

arouse them as you might a menhaden
or a mako shark, carefully but incessantly

determinedly, mightily, hungrily
for their flesh comes in a variety of colors

during the throes of passion, fishwives
come longer and louder, whose eggs salty like roe

but fewer and farther in-between
than fair weather-beaten vulva

for a taste of the esoteric, leave them then
on deck, naked beneath sun and spray

these welsh men and women are like
unbridled seahorses, you understand

before breeding, they may court for several days
and consummate their passion

over a period often to exceed eight hours
but never less than four or five

in porthmadog port, gelindy eifionidde
nearest chrysler, clanders, and dalgelu

hunting and fishing, the sea
and the products of aquaculture

of different kinds of flesh are farmed, but
an animal is denied, even if

you are an important source
of protein in many diets

consumed by humans, humans are animals
do not deny them, farm them

rejoice for he is on a plate, too
he is cut and filleted, he

is used in feed for fish

For the Penrhyndeudraeth Poetry Foundation Festival,
Portmeirion, Wales

96

fish swim in sand

fish swim in sand
fish understand
fish

no matter the reason
don't look for a reason
fish are their own reason

like love

love swims in sand
love understands
fish

brook this rivulet and swell this sea

brook this rivulet and swell this sea
arise, your hips, to set us free

for the hydrospherical embraces
both wail and fear the deep

vorticity sucks and exclamations chill
my love for you, minnow-sized, puckered

rather let me nibble and bite and chomp,
lick, love, taste, tongue, tickle, and sneeze, too

there's that cetacean who's gone boating
who's off the tracks, who's out to lunch with you

mad, crazy, wagging tail, senseless, and fou,
am i a big fish in a little pond

or a little pond in a big wish
ah-choo, chew, choo-choo choo

it's the anchovy who lurks

it's the anchovy who lurks
beside the rough sculpin

black patch over one eye
tin cup in twisted fin

begging for change for drink for salvation

fish sharks eat chase minnows

"When you fish for love, bait with your heart, not your brain."

fish sharks eat chase minnows
fish sharks eat *eat* minnows
fish sharks eat eat *fish*
fish *fish* eat eat fish

and
if

(as if *if* were enough)

fish fish *fish fish* fish

Opening quotation from
Notebook *(1898) by Mark Twain*

tell me what sort of fish you like
(susan lee)

No water is still, on top.
Without wind, even, it is full
Of a chill, superficial agitation.
It is easy to forget,
Or not to know at all.

tell me what sort of fish you like (susan lee)
tell me what animals rouse you from sleep
and
i'll tell you the passage
in the school yard
that leads to treasure
beyond the imaginings even of cod

for SLH

Opening epigraph from
"The Movement of Fish" by James Dickey

a pocketful of fish

after a dip into the sea
i dip a hand into me

a pocketful of fish, i find
a handful of water-kind

together tossed back into the sea
a half-dozen or so fishes set free

of light, and i wonder
have i just now saved your life?

or have you saved mine?
you know the sea prompts

when between classes are instances
when between classes are cigarettes and beer

and over the hill
under the sheets

the harelip sucker feeds with abandon
the harelip sucker no longer waits for you

that college girl, that briny coed, that salty scholar
that pupil of your eye

she no longer waits alone
she no longer waits

she denudes, decodes, delights
others

the escalation of fish

in life there is love
in shelters, or without
in life there is hope
when love falters, or fails
and
hope without boundaries
hope without reason
is like a sea without
the escalation of fish

mothers walk

mothers walk
and
mothers crumble
and
mothers talk
and
mothers rumble
and
mothers milk
joyous, humble

mothers smile
and
mothers cuddle
and
mothers wile
and
mothers huddle
and
mothers pile
pass and fumble

— *look out!*

that ball's really a unicorn tang!

you dream of a dance

a pestilence, a masque
you dream of a dance

you dream of a future
you dream in your pants

since that terrible day
votre amour a été perdu

ce fantôme
with a bright red eye

like a tancho koi harmonium,
like a pump organ,
plays here

when you said we must make love

when you said we must make love
i didn't know what you meant

at first. i thought we had plenty
of love already. too much, even.

still, i didn't mind the undressing
or the ritual copulation

the salty tongue, the mild gymnastics
the nails, the hammer, the screwdriver —

hold on. wait a second. what's all this for?

"at the bottom of a whirlpool, at the bottom of the sea,
a mobster tide," you soon replied

"will take you forever from me.
imagine thy doom's image," you said

"in the freshwater eye of a lonesome albacore.
imagine a lobster quadrille," you implied,

"that doesn't want to dance with you anymore."

will you hold my breath

will you hold my breath
for me
while i am away
watch it, keep it safe, make sure no one touches it
but you

will you hold your tongue
as i am yawning
your knees apart
and tickled pink a marbled headstander
licks the sleep from your reedy lips

will you come
to realize
in-between your moans and gasps
that a tickled pink marbled headstander
licks the sleep from your reedy lips

a bitter taste of stapled carp

a bitter taste of stapled carp

sushi, really

it was one of those days
when you say things you regret
when you say things, like

even when undressed
you're never naked, like

the mightiest cryptographers
can't decode your sweet nothings, like

you're the talking dead
the walking dead — dead, dead, dead, like

you can't cook sushi, really, you can't, you can't,
not without a helluva lot of nerve

loach goby hosts
a vegetarian thanksgiving

must i give thanks for
tuna cavalla mbuna and carp
tuna with grouper or tuna with oil
tuna with tuna tuna in doubt
tuna with goldfish blind tetra and trout
sábalo black guppy toado and roe
monkfish and tuna on tuna to go?

look me in the eyes, chicken of the sea:
i am the turkey, i am the turkey!

there are no reindeer fish

there are no reindeer fish
no fish in the snow
there are no fishnet stockings
without your fire's glow
there are no elves awash
in santa's soaring sleigh
there are no fish no fish no fish
no fish no fish, i say

there are fish in the sea

there are fish in the sea
there are fish in the air
in gardens are swans
not fish everywhere
in gardens are sheep
in gardens are lead
there are fish in the grass
there are fish i just said

pity this busy nunster poetry snot

pity this busy nunster poetry snot
pity the scribbler in afternoon church
and
hold out your hand
hold out for time
the cast of thousands will net abalone

For the half-centennial celebration of the publication of
Fifty Poems *by e. e. cummings, Columbia University*

sometimes weather threatens

sometimes weather
threatens
sometimes
whether doubts
sometimes ships fall
silent
sometimes kinsmen shout
sometimes winds sail smoothly
down high uncharted seas, and
sometimes fruits fall freely from your salmon-bearing trees

how death like perch

how like a trout am i
full of thunder and repose
how unlike a rose

to prefer dancers
to lovers, to seamen, to ports
perfection, of sorts

what is the worth of a man
who trades truth for the stillness of the deep
inside you

how death like perch

-ish

the f in fish is hardly silent
the end of fish, always sibilant
a fortune teller calls for silence

listen to the crash of surf on sand,
followed by its whisperèd retreat
and i am the whorl in between

i will follow your booming un-
happiness i will sing before your
hush of despair, neither bow nor bark

nor doubt, for if i am your lover
i'm not alone — me and mrs. jones
we're knee deep in your surf

so spread your sea-stained legs for mother
for my bondage is in the seafood
supply chain locked fast around your neck

and i am the icebreaker
the principal function of the fin
i help you to swim

from the jaws of death
unto the jaws of doom
there are more endings than you can know

dorsal fin, caudal fin, pectoral fin, go!
and when the seas are still
still i will look for signs of you

truth, justice, love, and sin
flipper, finger, bone, and fin–

About the Poet

Choo 3T Fish (b. 1928) is a Chinese American poet and neologist, credited with coining the phrase "iambic rentameter," originally to describe his own work. Born in China, but greatly influenced by his graduate studies at Harvard in the early 1960s, Mr. Fish is considered one of North America's most redoubtable poets. Although his work is not widely known, he has remained in print for over fifty years. His *Roe Roe Roe Your Boat* appeared in 1978 only four years after his third collection, *Swimming Through the Darkness*, won the National Poetry Award. He makes his home in Woods Hole, MA, and in Providence, RI, where he is *professor emeritus* at Brown University.

About the Editors

Tamara Croup is the Senior Archivist of the Special Collections Department of the John Hay Library at Brown University in Providence, RI; and Senior Lecturer in the university's Department of Contemporary Poetry. She holds a Ph.D. from Columbia University in English Literature and her graduate thesis, *Line by Line: Race Baiting and Casting Techniques in "they buried me uncooked,"* published in 2001, won the Kowitt Award for Critical Investigation. Since 2001, she has edited six poetry anthologies, including *Infirm Brightness* by Jean-Paul Halicalicali and *Black Is Right* by N. D. King. She is currently a visiting professor at Saint John University in Beirut, Lebanon, an apocryphal Christian institution where she teaches computational amoury and abstract formalism in the School of Arts and Letters.

Mark Malamud is the editor of *Descent: The Journal of Ichthyopathic Poetry*, and a regular contributor to *A Babel of Waves*, the Choo 3T Fish newsletter. His collection of stories, *The Gymnasium*, established the idea of literary taxidermy. His most-recent novel, *The Timeless Machine*, reworks H. G. Wells' classic novella to explore the limitations and contradictions of living with grief.

Other Books by Mark Malamud

The Timeless Machine

The place is Richmond, a suburb of London. And something terrible — or wonderful — has happened. A scientist, known only as the Time Traveler, has invented an antidote for grief.

On the Orient Express

By altering an event early in Agatha Christie's mystery—this time there is no murder—the remaining text must re-adjust to accommodate the absence of the crime.

The Gymnasium

Nineteen tales of melancholy and wonder created by "re-stuffing" what goes in-between the opening and closing lines of classic works by Milan Kundera, Philip K. Dick, Thomas Wolfe, and others.

124 Beloved

An anthology of literary taxidermy based on the first and last lines of *Beloved* by Toni Morrison. Award-winning stories from the 2020 Literary Taxidermy Short Story Competition, edited by Mark Malamud

Labiovelora

When Professor Alain Sapiens meets Vessel Giselle Cinnamoana he Miscegenatura, there's more than romance in the air. There's thunder, lightning, and the definite tang of oblivion.

www.regulus.press

www.ingramcontent.com/pod-product-compliance
Lightning Source LLC
LaVergne TN
LVHW091156080426
835509LV00006B/706